55

Ways to be
Blessed
and Not Stressed

55

Ways to be

Blessed

and Not Stressed

JOEL OSTEEN

Contents

Introduction

This book is in your hands on purpose. God doesn't want you to be stressed when He created you to be blessed!

The thing is, you can't enjoy all the blessings God wants to give you if you are overwhelmed with stress. As you learn how to stress less, you will start receiving and enjoying the blessings that God has promised to you. There are certainly more than 55 ways to be blessed and less stressed. So you might be thinking, *why 55*?

The Bible shows us that numbers are significant. On the seventh day of creation, God rested; seven is the number of completion. For 40 days, Jesus fasted in the desert; forty represents a time of testing. Jesus took five loaves of bread to feed 5,000 people; five is the number of God's grace and goodness.

Grace is God's goodness and favor given to each one of us. (See Ephesians 4:7.) You can't earn it. You don't deserve it. As a child of Almighty God, He simply gives His grace freely and abundantly to you.

When you believe you were created to live in God's goodness and grace, you will think about it, you will talk about it, you will walk in it, and you will continually receive it and see it manifest in your life.

As you receive these 55 ways to be blessed into your heart and life, the weight of worry will fall off of you and you will begin to see God's grace in every area of your life. Healing, favor, joy, and abundance are waiting for you. God wants you to receive His grace so that you can be blessed and less stressed!

In faith,

Receive and enjoy the blessings that God has promised to you.

1

Look for Streams in the Desert

Just because you don't feel favored doesn't mean you're not favored. You might feel stuck or stressed, but God is always with you and He'll do something amazing just to remind you He's in control. Isaiah 35:6 says that God will make *"streams in the desert"* (NIV). A stream in a lush green land would be lovely, but a stream in the desert can only be God. That's the kind of unconventional blessing He wants to bring to your life — when you least expect it, when it doesn't make sense, when you didn't see it coming. If you are in a desert season, or just feeling stuck, stay encouraged. Streams of living water will burst forth!

Praise be to the God and Father of our Lord Jesus Christ, who has blessed us in the heavenly realms with every spiritual blessing in Christ.
EPHESIANS 1:3, NIV

2

Start a Blessing

There's something called a generational blessing. Just like negative traits sometimes get passed down, how much more the positive! When you make decisions that honor God, when you're generous, when you're faithful, your life is not only going to be more rewarding, but that obedience is being credited to your children's account, to your grandchildren, to future generations. Your descendants will see favor and victory because you started an avalanche of blessing. Knowing this, make the decision today to honor God in your relationships, your finances, your career, and your spiritual life, and start a generational blessing in your family today.

But I lavish unfailing love for a thousand generations on those who love me and obey my commands.
EXODUS 20:6, NLT

3

This Too
Shall Pass

Once, on a 15-hour flight to India, my plane hit major turbulence. For about 10 minutes it was utter chaos. Eventually everything calmed down, and the rest of the flight was as peaceful as can be. This is how it is in life. Everything is smooth sailing and then turbulence hits — an unexpected challenge, a sickness, a layoff, a betrayal — and we're tempted to panic. But let me encourage you: it's just part of your 10 minutes of turbulence. It's not going to last. Trust that God has it already figured out, and the rest of your flight is going to be smooth sailing.

Blessed is the one who perseveres under trial because, having stood the test, that person will receive the crown of life that the Lord has promised to those who love him.

JAMES 1:12, NIV

4

Equipped in the Battle

After the Israelites were living in the promised land, the Scripture says God left some of their enemies in the land. *"He did this to teach warfare to generations of Israelites who had no experience in battle"* (Judges 3:2, NLT). If God had wiped out all the opposition, the new generation of Israelites would have eventually faced armies and been defeated because they didn't have battle experience. God had to toughen them up, so He left obstacles on purpose. God has amazing things in your future, but you won't get there if you're not equipped. Trust that God is strengthening you through difficult and uncomfortable situations. When you face resistance and have to stretch, you're being prepared for blessings ahead.

But blessed is the one who trusts in the LORD, whose confidence is in him.
JEREMIAH 17:7, NIV

5

Disconnect from Discord

You won't reach the fullness of your destiny if you surround yourself with people who constantly stir up trouble. That's why Paul used such strong language in Romans 16:17, *"I urge you, brothers and sisters, to watch out for those who cause divisions . . ."* (NIV). He was saying, *I beg you, I implore you, I challenge you* — "stay away!" Don't let them poison your spirit. Don't let that discord get in you. If someone is constantly disgruntled, jealous, and bringing division, recognize they are not for you. Don't let them bring their stress into your life. Be kind and be respectful, but you don't have to let them in.

I urge you, brothers and sisters, to watch out for those who cause divisions and put obstacles in your way that are contrary to the teaching you have learned. Keep away from them.

ROMANS 16:17, NIV

6

Change Your Course

His whole life, Jacob had been dishonest. When he finally got tired of living this way, he went down to the brook to get alone with God. That night he wrestled with the Lord and an angel said, *"Your name will no longer be Jacob,"* which means trickster. *"From now on you will be called Israel,"* which means prince of God (Genesis 32:28, NLT). Jacob left there, not only with a new name but also with a new attitude and a new passion to do the right thing. It is never too late to change your course. When you choose to let go of the past, and the person you were, the stressors that accompanied you will fall off. A new season of blessing is waiting for you.

"Then the man said, 'Your name will no longer be Jacob, but Israel, because you have struggled with God and with humans and have overcome.'"
GENESIS 32:28, NIV

7

Think Power
Thoughts

Proverbs 4:23 says, *"Be careful what you think, because your thoughts run your life"* (NCV). Are your thoughts helping you or adding more stress? It's easy to go around thinking that the obstacle is too big, we'll never get well, this relationship will never work. We wonder why we don't have any strength and why we can't get ahead. It's because our thoughts are limiting us! We will become what we constantly think about. Instead of thinking weak, defeated, stressed out thoughts, start thinking power thoughts: "Favor is surrounding me like a shield. No weapon formed against me will prosper. Goodness and mercy are following me." Knowing that victory starts in the mind, start thinking power thoughts!

———————————⌄———————————

Now thanks be to God who always leads us in triumph in Christ, and through us diffuses the fragrance of His knowledge in every place.
2 CORINTHIANS 2:14, NKJV

8

God is Up to Something

You don't have to fight everything that comes your way. In fact, you can trust that God fights your battles on your behalf. If you're being falsely accused, if someone seems to be standing in your way, if you are in the middle of a stressful storm, God will use it all for your good and His glory. If that adversity was going to stop your destiny, God wouldn't have allowed it. If that disappointment was going to keep you from your purpose, it wouldn't have happened. If God didn't stop that trial from coming, it's because God is up to something. Keep being your best even when it's not fair. Stop resisting and start trusting that He is ordering your steps. You are blessed!

————————————————⌄————————————————

But I tell you not to resist an evil person. But whoever slaps you on your right cheek, turn the other to him also.
MATTHEW 5:39, NKJV

9

Blessing In and Out of Season

God specializes in doing things out of season. He doesn't wait for the conditions to be perfect, for the circumstances to line up, for the right people to believe in you. He does things unexpectedly, when you didn't see it coming. Sarah gave birth to a baby at 90. David was a teenager with no royal training when he was anointed the next king of Israel. The season seemed too late for Sarah and too early for David, but not for God. If you are out of season, don't let that stress you; begin to believe that you are in prime position for God to show out in your life!

Preach the word; be prepared in season and out of season; correct, rebuke and encourage—with great patience and careful instruction.
2 TIMOTHY 4:2, NIV

10

Keep Calm and Rule the Day

The Scripture says that God has given you the power to keep calm in the days of trouble (see Psalm 94:13, NIV). It doesn't say the power to avoid adversity or to not have challenges, but to keep calm when trouble comes. When trouble comes, you don't have to get upset. When plans don't work out, you don't have to let the stress get to you. When someone is rude, you don't have to get offended. When blessings are delayed, you don't have to fret over what is taking so long. You are positioned to choose, and you have the power to remain calm and rule the day by controlling your thoughts, attitudes, and emotions. God did not bring you this far to leave you. Trust that if the enemy is trying to stop you, it is because there is something awesome coming right around the corner.

You grant them relief from days of trouble, till a pit is dug for the wicked.
PSALM 94:13, NIV

11

Expect God's Goodness

We've all gone through something that we thought would be the end of us. We couldn't imagine any way out. But the reason you can't see how it's going to happen is because God is going to do it in an unconventional way. We think we have to give God all the details in case He's not sure how to answer our prayers, but really all we need to do is sit back and expect God's goodness. The answer will come when you didn't see it coming. It won't happen the way you thought. It will be better than what you expected! So relax, send the stress away, expect God's goodness, and let Him do it His way.

"My thoughts are nothing like your thoughts," says the LORD. "And my ways are far beyond anything you could imagine."
ISAIAH 55:8, NLT

12

Sing in
the Storm

In Acts 16, we read that Paul and Silas were arrested for sharing their faith and put in the inner dungeon. They were locked behind prison doors with chains around their feet. Sounds awful! Yet, at midnight, they started singing praises to God. As a child of Almighty God, storms don't have to send you into a stressful spiral. No! When you can sing in the storm, when you can praise through the pain, when you can thank God He's working rather than complain, get ready. Your miracle is on the way. The Scripture says, *"Suddenly, there was a massive earthquake"* (Acts 16:26, NLT). The prison was shaken, doors flung open, and chains fell off their feet. If you'll start singing in your storm, you can believe that your "suddenly" is coming!

They replied, "Believe in the Lord Jesus and you will be saved, along with everyone in your household."
ACTS 16:31, NLT

13

Get in Agreement

When you speak negative words over your life, they muddy your mind and impact your heart. You weren't meant to live with that negativity and stress. When you speak positive words of faith, you get in agreement with God and miracles begin to happen! Matthew 18:19, NLT says, *"If two of you agree here on earth concerning anything you ask, my Father in heaven will do it for you."* Get in agreement with God and what His Word says about you and speak positive words of faith: "I am the head and not the tail; I am a child of Almighty God, favor finds me, stress has to leave me, I am blessed beyond measure." Receive the promises of God over your life.

———————————⌄———————————

And whatever you do, whether in word or deed, do it all in the name of the Lord Jesus, giving thanks to God the Father through him.
COLOSSIANS 3:17, NIV

14

The Commanded Blessing

Deuteronomy 28:8 says, *"The LORD will command the blessing on you"* (NKJV). When God commands, it's not a "maybe." It's not an "I hope." It's an absolute. The earth was dark, without form, like a black hole. But when God commanded light, it came at 186,000 miles per second. In the same way, when God commands you to be blessed, it doesn't matter what family you come from, where you work, or how good the economy is that year. When He commands the blessing, all the forces of darkness cannot stop it, and the worry and stress have to leave you. Trust that the commanded blessing on your life will override any force that is trying to hold you back.

"The LORD will guarantee a blessing on everything you do and will fill your storehouses with grain. The LORD your God will bless you in the land he is giving you."
DEUTERONOMY 28:8, NLT

15

Don't Get
Stuck There

What you believe in times of trouble will determine whether you come out or whether you get stuck there. Job went through great difficulty. When he looked at all that he'd lost, he got depressed. He sat down in the ashes and wanted to die. But then he changed his attitude. He got up out of those ashes, looked heavenward and said, *"I know that my Redeemer lives"* (Job 19:25, NLT). God shows us both sides of Job to tell us it's okay to feel things. It's okay to be discouraged. It's okay to start there, but don't finish there. At some point, you have to get out of the ashes and declare: "I know that my Redeemer lives!"

"But as for me, I know that my Redeemer lives, and he will stand upon the earth at last."
JOB 19:25, NLT

16

Keep Doing the Right Thing

I know a young man who was a hard worker. He always did more than he had to do, but his supervisor didn't like him. For six years this young man worked an entry-level position while less qualified individuals got promoted over him. It wasn't fair, but he kept doing his job. He kept working hard. He kept doing the right thing. Then, one day, his supervisor unexpectedly resigned. Management called in the young man and said his supervisor had recommended he take over. The supervisor didn't even like him, but people don't have the final say; God does. Don't stress over things that are outside your control. Keep doing the right thing, and God can even use your enemies to bless you!

The LORD said to my Lord, "Sit in the place of honor at my right hand until I humble your enemies, making them a footstool under your feet."
PSALM 110:1, NLT

17

Tune In
With God

Psalm 125:4, NLT says, *"O Lord, do good to those who are good, whose hearts are in tune with you,"* Keep your heart in tune with God and what His Word says. Negative, depressed thinking is not in tune with God. The way to get in tune is by thinking victorious, overcoming, faith-filled thoughts. Nowhere in the Scripture does it say that God is weak, discouraged, afraid, unable, or unwilling. When Moses asked God what His name was, God said, "I Am." He was saying, I am everything. I am strength. I am healing. I am provision, I am abundance. I am protection. I am favor. Stress and sadness are not yours to carry. Tune in with God by thinking the way God thinks about you!

———————————⋁———————————

"Seek the Kingdom of God above all else, and live righteously, and he will give you everything you need."
MATTHEW 6:33, NLT

18

Stay at
Rest

Hebrews 4:3, NLT says, *"For only we who believe can enter his rest."* When you're at rest, you're in faith. You're showing God that you trust Him. That's what allows God to work. If you're upset over what's not changing, worried about your finances, and can't sleep because your child is off course, that's a sign you've stopped believing. You can't trust God and be worried at the same time. When you're at rest, you're not stressed! You know God is in control, you know all things are going to work for your good, and you know what He started He will finish. Pray, believe, enter His rest, and stay at rest!

Cast all your anxiety on him because he cares for you.
1 PETER 5:7, NIV

19

The Voice of
the Lord

You may have a lot coming against you, but if you keep obeying the voice of the Lord, God will bring vindication, justice, and deliverance. He's going to bring increase, abundance, and cause doors to open that bring you to the next level. Freedom, wholeness, and breakthrough are yours. Those addictions, those bad habits, the stress weighing on you are not your destiny. God is bringing healing, restoration, and strength. It may not have happened yet. But this is a new day. *"And all these blessings shall come upon you and overtake you, because you obey the voice of the LORD your God"* (Deuteronomy 28:2, NKJV).

———————————⌄———————————

Now this is the confidence that we have in Him, that if we ask anything according to His will, He hears us.
1 JOHN 5:14, NKJV

20

Receive

His Favor

When Ruth moved to Bethlehem with her mother-in-law, Naomi, God granted her favor with a field owner named Boaz who welcomed her to glean in his fields. Long story short, she ended up marrying him. She no longer worked in the field; now she owned the field. If your situation looks hopeless, remember Ruth — a poor widow, a stranger in a foreign land, who received the favor of God. You can stress less, knowing that your circumstances are no match for God's blessings. If you could see where God was going to take you, it would boggle your mind; but you can rest assured that His favor will take you there. (See Ruth 2:10.)

Surely, LORD, you bless the righteous; you surround them with your favor as with a shield.

PSALM 5:12, NIV

21

Shake

It Off

Nothing you've done is a surprise to God. He knew every mistake you would make. You can still get to where you're supposed to be, but you have to shake off the guilt and move ahead. Quit telling yourself that you've made too many mistakes. No more living guilty and condemned. Paul said in 2 Corinthians 5:21, *"For God made Christ, who never sinned, to be the offering for our sin, so that we could be made right with God through Christ"* (NLT). He became what He wasn't so we could become who we were created to be. Now whoever looks up to the Son and believes in Him will live. There is freedom for you as you shake it off and look up. You have been made right with God.

―――――――――――⌄―――――――――――

For it is by grace you have been saved, through faith— and this is not from yourselves, it is the gift of God.
EPHESIANS 2:8, NIV

22

Trust God's Timing

Once you pray, once you believe, you have to leave how God does it — and when He does it — up to Him. If you put a time frame on it and a method of how it's going to happen, you're going to stress, be frustrated, and have a hard time enjoying anything in your life. God is working when we can't see it. Sometimes it's taking longer because He has something better in store. One of the best things I've learned is to trust God's timing and trust His ways. The blessings God has promised will come to pass. You have to release control. Release having to have it happen your way and trust God's timing.

The Lord is not slow in keeping his promise, as some understand slowness. Instead he is patient with you, not wanting anyone to perish, but everyone to come to repentance.
2 PETER 3:9, NIV

23

Obey
in Full

One reason King Saul lost the throne was because he only obeyed God in part. When Samuel confronted him about it, Saul said, *"Yes, I have sinned. I have disobeyed your instructions and the LORD's command, for I was afraid of the people and did what they demanded"* (1 Samuel 15:24, NLT). Saul knew the right things to do, but he didn't want to disappoint the people. You can't be a people pleaser and reach your potential. Don't let the fear of what people are going to think stress you out. Take advice and listen to wise counsel, but ultimately you'll have to do what God says.

Jesus replied, "Anyone who loves me will obey my teaching. My Father will love them, and we will come to them and make our home with them.
JOHN 14:23, NIV

24

God is

Working

48

You can find joy right where you are and trust God will get you to where you want to be. If you believe that you can only be happy when the problem turns around, when you get married, when you have the baby, when your business grows, when you retire, that will keep you from the blessings you are meant to receive today. It is good to be passionate about your dreams, passionate to see healing, freedom, and promotion, but don't be so consumed that you're not going to be happy while you're waiting for God to bring it to pass. That will add unnecessary stress to your life. This day is a gift. Enjoy your life while God is working.

The LORD has done it this very day; let us rejoice today and be glad.
PSALM 118:24, NIV

25

Along the Way

God uses closed doors just as much as open doors. He uses rejection, betrayal, and delays to position us for promotion. Joseph had a dream. He knew God's favor was on him. But he was betrayed by his brothers, thrown into a pit, sold into slavery, had to work in a foreign country, was falsely accused, and put in prison. All of these bad breaks and lonely nights, however, moved him to his destiny. Proverbs 20:24, NLT says, *"The LORD directs our steps, so why try to understand everything along the way?"* If you're trying to figure everything out, you're going to get confused. There are things you aren't supposed to understand. That's what faith is all about! Don't let the setbacks bring stress into your life. You are blessed and God is using everything in your favor!

The LORD directs the steps of the godly. He delights in every detail of their lives.
PSALM 37:23, NLT

26

Get a New

Perspective

What God has blessed, nothing can curse. When the enemy tells you all the reasons why you're not going to get well, not get out of debt, not overcome that challenge, instead of letting stress get the best of you, allow God to give you a new perspective. The enemy wants you to curse your future with negative words and negative thinking. He knows he can't stop you, but if he can convince you to live stressed out and discouraged, thinking you've reached your limits, then that will keep you from your destiny. When you get a new perspective and understand that every force trying to stop you is powerless to change the blessing on your life, you can start expecting victory, favor, health, and abundance. (See Numbers 22:12.)

And the peace of God, which transcends all understanding, will guard your hearts and your minds in Christ Jesus.
PHILIPPIANS 4:7, NIV

27

Release Your Burden

Psalm 55:22 says, *"Cast your burden on the Lord [releasing the weight of it] and He will sustain you"* (AMPC). How many weights are you carrying around? The weight of stress, the weight of what you don't understand, the weight of fear, frustration, family, finances . . . God will carry those burdens for you, but first you have to release them. Release the worry, release the frustration, release the need to figure it out. Come back to a place of peace. If you'll release your burden, I believe and declare the weights that have kept you down are lifting off of you right now. Let God bless you by releasing all your burdens to Him today.

"For I am the LORD your God who takes hold of your right hand and says to you, Do not fear; I will help you."
ISAIAH 41:13, NIV

28

Rule Your

Atmosphere

Proverbs 25:28 says, *"He who has no rule over his own spirit is like a city that is broken down and without walls"* (AMPC). In Bible times, the walls protected the city, so if the walls were down, anyone could get in and take the city. In the same way, if you don't rule your atmosphere and put up some boundaries, then everything is going to get in, weigh you down, and stress you out. You weren't meant for that! Your atmosphere is comprised of your thoughts, attitude, emotions, who you spend time with, and what you watch and listen to. Your time is too valuable and your assignment too important to let everything in. Be selective. If it's not positive, hopeful, and of a good report, then don't let it in!

———————————⌄———————————

Commit everything you do to the LORD. Trust him, and he will help you.
PSALM 37:5, NLT

29

Blessed

Relationships

Are your friends making you better, inspiring you, challenging you to go further, or are they pulling you down, causing you to compromise, and bringing out the worst in you? Who you spend time with is so important because you will become like the people you hang around. God will send the right people in your life — blessed relationships that build you up. He'll bring you divine connections — people who will help propel you forward and help you reach your destiny. Take some time to thoughtfully evaluate your friendships.

Whoever walks with the wise becomes wise, but the companion of fools will suffer harm.

PROVERBS 13:20, ESV

30

Hold Your Peace

Exodus 14:14 says, *"The LORD will fight for you, and you shall hold your peace"* (NKJV). You may be in a situation that's unfair — somebody did you wrong, you're dealing with an illness, you went through a loss. You could be worried, bitter, and upset, but that won't make what happened go away. This is where you have to do like David — when Saul was tracking him down and trying to kill him — and dig down deep and say, *"I wait for you to rescue me, for you, O God, are my fortress. In his unfailing love, my God will stand with me"* (Psalm 59:9–10, NLT). The way to be blessed, and less stressed, is to hold your peace and let God fight your battles.

"You shall not fear them, for it is the LORD your God who fights for you."
DEUTERONOMY 3:22, ESV

61

31

Embrace

Where

You Are

God doesn't always take us down a straight path. There will be detours, delays, curves, and times when you feel like you're going in the wrong direction. What you can't see is, there is a turn ahead — a shortcut that will catapult you further down the right path than if you had gone straight away. Psalm 102:13 says there is a "set time" (NKJV) — a set time for favor, a set time for healing, a set time to turn the problem around. If there's a right time, that means there's a wrong time. You will create stress for yourself when you try to make something happen that hasn't come to its set time. Embrace where you are. Trust that God is ordering your steps, and your set time for blessing is coming.

I know, O LORD, that the way of man is not in himself, that it is not in man who walks to direct his steps.
JEREMIAH 10:23, ESV

32

Have a
Good Day

Every day can be a good day. Quit waiting for all the circumstances to be perfect. You can even have a good day in the middle of a hardship. You can have a good day even though you have challenges at work, in your health, or your family. The apostle Paul told Timothy to "be calm and cool and steady" whether he was having a good day or a hard day, whether he was welcomed or not welcomed, whether it was convenient or inconvenient (2 Timothy 4:5, AMPC). Decide before your feet even hit the floor in the morning that no matter what comes your way you are going to stress less, be blessed, and have a good day!

But you be watchful in all things, endure afflictions, do the work of an evangelist, fulfill your ministry.
2 TIMOTHY 4:5, NKJV

33

Shine Your

Light

As a child of Almighty God, you are set apart. You're a difference maker. People can see your influence, your gifts, and the favor on your life. The higher you get, the brighter you shine your light. But also, the more visible you are, the more opportunities there will be for people to misunderstand who you are and what you are about. Don't veer off course. Stay humble, be honoring, but don't let what others do or think hold you back. Don't let yourself stress out about others' opinions. It's not really about you anyway. It's about the blessing God put on you. If you want to fulfill your destiny, don't take what others say personally.

Do not let any unwholesome talk come out of your mouths, but only what is helpful for building others up according to their needs, that it may benefit those who listen.
EPHESIANS 4:29, NIV

34

While You
Wait

When we go through challenges in life, it's easy to live worried and stressed. We wonder when it's going to change and when God is going to do something — when, in fact, God is doing something! We don't realize it but we're in the middle of a miracle. God is in the process of bringing us out. Right now, God is working behind the scenes making things happen that you can't see. If it weren't for His goodness, His favor, His mercy, you wouldn't be able to withstand what's trying to stop you. While you wait, remember: You're not in this difficulty by yourself. God is pushing back forces of darkness right now on your behalf!

But Jesus replied, "My Father is always working, and so am I."
JOHN 5:17, NLT

35

Have a "Soon" Mentality

Paul said in 2 Corinthians 4, *"Our present troubles are small and won't last very long . . . For the things we see now will soon be gone"* (vv. 17–18, NLT). What you're up against may look permanent, but Paul reminds us not to be fooled by what we see — they will "soon be gone." Instead of thinking of all the reasons why it will "never" work out, have a "soon" mentality: soon I'll get well; soon I'll meet the right person; soon this problem is going to turn around. When you have this soon mentality, you can wake up with expectancy, knowing that this could be the day that God shows out in your life.

For everything there is a season, a time for every activity under heaven.

ECCLESIASTES 3:1, NLT

36

Your Miracle in Motion

When Moses sent 12 spies into the promised land, Joshua and Caleb came back saying, *"We are well able"* (Numbers 13:30, NKJV). That report didn't go anywhere. When the other 10 spies came back saying they were no match for the giants, who were too strong and powerful to be defeated, that news spread like wildfire throughout the camp. Negative thinking is contagious. But Isaiah 8:11, NLT says, *"The Lord has given me a strong warning not to think like everyone else does."* Don't think like the 10 spies. When the majority is afraid, remember that God repeatedly says, "Do not be afraid." When you believe what God says, you set your miracle in motion.

"For with God nothing will be impossible."
LUKE 1:37, NKJV

37

It is Still

Coming

Job went through forty-two chapters of despair, but the final two verses of his story say, "After this *Job lived one hundred and forty years, and saw his children and grandchildren for four generations. So Job died, old and full of days*" (Job 42:16–17, NKJV). Don't be discouraged by the trouble you are going through. It's not stopping anything God has for you. What belongs to you is still coming your way. Your latter days will be better than your former days. *After this*, there's going to be great joy in your life. *After this*, you're going to see new friendships, new opportunities, new growth. *Believe* that God has already lined up an "after this." Your breakthrough and blessing are coming!

You too, be patient and stand firm, because the Lord's coming is near.
JAMES 5:8, NIV

38

Stay Open for Something Great

If you could see what God is up to, you wouldn't be stressed. Many times, a great upset precedes great favor; great difficulty precedes great promotion; great opposition precedes great influence. When you realize that the disruption is taking you to a place where you're going to flourish and do things you've never dreamed of, you would thank God even when you are shaken. Even though it's uncertain, you can have a smile on your face and a spring in your step, knowing that God is up to something good. Now is not the time to fall apart. Now is the time to kick your praise into high gear and stay open for something great!

"See, I am doing a new thing! Now it springs up; do you not perceive it? I am making a way in the wilderness and streams in the wasteland."
ISAIAH 43:19, NIV

39

Seek Him First

Proverbs 13:22 says, *"The wealth of the sinner is laid up for the just"* (KJV). There are things God has laid up for you. There is going to be a transfer of blessing, from people who only think about themselves to people who will use their resources to build the Kingdom, to lift the fallen, to feed the hungry, to bring justice to those who have no voice, and to make the world a better place. God is about to shift things in your favor. It's just a matter of time before you see God do unprecedented things. You don't have to seek the blessing; seek Him first and the blessings will seek you.

"You will seek me and find me when you seek me with all your heart."

JEREMIAH 29:13, NIV

40
Invite God In

Sometimes the miracle is not in getting *out*; it's in what God is going to do in the situation. Most of the time we pray, "God, get me out of this!" But what is even more powerful than God bringing you out is when God comes in and begins to change things. If you're only focused on God bringing you out, then you're going to be stressed and frustrated until your situation changes. When you ask God to come in, then you can have peace while you wait. Invite God in — into the hospital room, into the office, into your anxiety, into your marriage. He's waiting for your invitation.

———————————⌄———————————

Even though I walk through the darkest valley, I will fear no evil, for you are with me; your rod and your staff, they comfort me.
PSALM 23:4, NIV

41
Turn It Up

In the Scripture, three Hebrew teenagers wouldn't bow down to the king's golden idol. The king threatened to throw them into a fiery furnace. The teenagers said they weren't worried. This made the king even more angry, so he ordered the guards to turn up the heat. Sometimes God is not bringing you out yet because He wants the odds to be against you in a bigger way. Then, when He brings you out, it's a greater miracle. The teenagers told the king, "Turn it up, we know our God will deliver us." *"But even if he doesn't,"* they said, *". . . we will never serve your gods"* (Daniel 3:18, NLT). Even when your troubles are turned up or life feels turned upside down, keep worshiping God through it all, and watch as you are untouched and unharmed by the hardship.

Worship the LORD with gladness; come before him with joyful songs.
PSALM 100:2, NIV

42

Don't Settle for Less

Maybe the reason you're not seeing God's blessing is because you've settled. You've accepted an okay job, an okay relationship, okay health. You think you'll never get out of debt, that your dream will never come true. As long as you think that way, it will limit your life. Instead, you need to know that mediocrity is not your home. Good enough is not your destiny. Getting by is not where you belong. You may be there now, but that is not your permanent location. If you're going to become all you were created to be, you have to make up your mind that you are blessed, and you're not going to settle for less than what God promised you.

———————————⌄———————————

"May the LORD, the God of your ancestors, increase you a thousand times and bless you as he has promised!"
DEUTERONOMY 1:11, NIV

43

Pick Your

Battles

Your time is too valuable to be stressed about what other people think about you. Everyone is not going to like you. Everyone is not going to accept you. Quit wasting time trying to convince someone to understand you if they are determined to misunderstand you. It takes discipline to say, "I'm not going to respond. I'm not going to sink down. I'm not going to waste my energy. I have a destiny to fulfill." When someone or something comes against you, ask yourself, "Will this battle propel me into my destiny?" If not, it's simply a distraction and not a battle worth fighting. Proverbs 20:3, NLT says, *"Avoiding a fight is a mark of honor."* Do the honorable thing. Honor God, be your best, and He'll get you to where you're supposed to be. Your victorious destiny awaits as you win the battle within!

Avoiding a fight is a mark of honor; only fools insist on quarreling.
PROVERBS 20:3, NLT

44
Letting Go

In Acts 27, Paul was a prisoner on a ship sailing toward Rome. A huge storm came, and the crew could not keep control of the ship. Instead of battling the storm, the scripture says they took down the sails and let the winds blow the ship wherever the storm wanted it to go. When you've done everything you can — you've prayed, you've believed, you've stood in faith — there comes a time where you have to quit fighting it; quit trying to force it to work out; quit losing sleep over it; and let go of control. Send all that stress away from you! Take down the sails, and trust that what the devil meant for harm, God will turn to your advantage.

———————⌄———————

Don't worry about anything; instead, pray about everything. Tell God what you need, and thank him for all he has done.
PHILIPPIANS 4:6, NLT

45

Turn to Your Shepherd

When we look at all that's going on in the world, it's easy to be worried and afraid. If you were on your own, you would have a reason to live stressed. But the scripture says, ". . . *now you have turned to your Shepherd, the Guardian of your souls*" (1 Peter 2:25, NLT). You're not in this by yourself. You have a Protector, a Defender, a Deliverer. He has protected you from things you know nothing about. He's been guarding your soul since you were born. If you knew all the things He's already kept you from, you wouldn't worry about what you're facing now. Turn to your Shepherd and stay in peace, knowing that you're in the palm of His hand.

"For the LORD your God is living among you. He is a mighty savior. He will take delight in you with gladness. With his love, he will calm all your fears. He will rejoice over you with joyful songs."
ZEPHANIAH 3:17, NLT

46

Stay in Faith

We read in 1 John 3:8, NLT, *"The Son of God came to destroy the works of the devil."* The word *destroy* in the original language means, "to not have its intended purpose." When the enemy attacks, the purpose is to take you out. But because God destroyed the works of the enemy, that attack is not going to destroy you. That divorce, the betrayal, the slowdown in the economy could sour your life, but God has other plans. We can't pray away every difficulty, but when you realize it's not going to have its intended purpose, then you can stay in faith. Don't let yourself be stressed when your identity is blessed! Keep thanking God that what was meant for harm, He is turning to your advantage.

———————————⌄———————————

Jesus looked at them and said, "With man this is impossible, but not with God; all things are possible with God."
MARK 10:27, NIV

47

Don't Answer
the Door

Difficulties may come, but they don't have to stay. Don't open the door to troubles and say, "I knew you'd show up. Come on in! Let me get you a cup of coffee." No. When opposition comes knocking, say, "No thanks, you're not welcome here." Don't accept it. Don't learn to live with it. Quit calling it "my" sickness, "my" anxiety, "my" dysfunction, "my" addiction. It's not yours. None of it belongs to you. Your body is a temple of the Most High God. Stress, sickness, depression, fear, addiction, lack — none of it belongs in your temple.

When I am afraid, I put my trust in you.
PSALM 56:3, NIV

48

Say of
the Lord

Psalm 91 starts off by saying, *"He who dwells in the secret place of the Most High shall abide under the shadow of the Almighty"* (v. 1, NKJV). The next verse says, *"I will say of the LORD, 'He is my refuge and my fortress; My God, in Him I will trust'"* (v. 2, NKJV). It's significant that the psalmist didn't just say, "I'm going to stay here, and God will keep me safe." He said, "I will say of the Lord . . ." What you say makes a difference. If you're talking defeat, zip it up. Start saying of the Lord, "Thank you for anointing me, for hiding me, for rescuing me, for bringing me out of this untouched." Your words will provoke God's blessings!

Come, let us sing for joy to the LORD; let us shout aloud to the Rock of our salvation.
PSALM 95:1, NIV

49

Protect Your Interior

A ship doesn't sink because of the water around it. A ship can be in a huge ocean, surrounded by hundreds of miles of water on every side. Water around it is not a problem. But if that ship lets what's on the outside get inside, then it's a problem. The same is true in your life. Sometimes, we are surrounded by negative voices — from the news, social media, coworkers, even family and friends — tempting us to worry and stress about every big and little thing — things way beyond our control. Those things will always be around us, but they don't have to affect us. You can protect your interior by keeping the negative out. (See Romans 12:2.) You are meant to be blessed, not stressed!

And give no opportunity to the devil.
EPHESIANS 4:27, ESV

50

The Size of
Your God

Life may be tough now, but 2 Corinthians 2:14 says, *"Now thanks be to God who always leads us in triumph"* (NKJV, emphasis added). Not some of the time. Not most of the time. But ALWAYS — all of the time, He causes us to triumph. The giants may be big, but our God is bigger. The obstacle may be high, but our God is the Most High. The opposition may be powerful, but our God is all-powerful. He parted seas. He closed the mouths of lions. He brought the dead back to life. Any time you are tempted to feel overwhelmed by life's obstacles, stop looking at how big the problem is, and look at the size of your God!

———————————⌄———————————

"They will fight against you but will not overcome you, for I am with you and will rescue you," declares the Lord.

JEREMIAH 1:19, NIV

51

Debts You Don't Owe

Romans 13:8 says, *"Owe no one anything except to love one another"* (NKJV). The only thing you really owe anyone is to love them. If you go around with a false sense of responsibility, thinking you have to keep everyone happy and letting people put their demands on you, you are carrying a debt that you don't owe — and you will be weighed down by stress. Always be respectful and kind, but don't go through life trying to please everyone. If you try to keep everyone happy, the one person who won't be happy is you. Come out from under that debt. Be kind. Go the extra mile. But remember that you don't owe anyone anything except to love them.

Let no debt remain outstanding, except the continuing debt to love one another, for whoever loves others has fulfilled the law.

ROMANS 13:8, NIV

52

Keep Pedaling

I have a bike route that I like to take. Most of the route is flat, but there is one very big hill. Normally I enjoy the challenge. One particular day, however, I was tired. Immediately I started dreading that hill. Then I received a phone call. We talked for about twenty minutes while I kept pedaling, but as soon as I hung up, I started dreading that hill again. When I looked around, however, I realized I had already gone up it! When we dread the hills in life, we drain our strength, but when we take our eyes off the problem, we realize God has already equipped us to handle everything that comes our way!

May he equip you with all you need for doing his will. May he produce in you, through the power of Jesus Christ, every good thing that is pleasing to him.
HEBREWS 13:21, NLT

53

Know That

He is God

Most of the time when you're in the middle of a miracle, it's not peaceful. In fact, it may look like all hell is breaking loose. Imagine how the Israelites must have felt when they saw 20-foot high walls of water on either side of them. They weren't calm and collected; they were terrified! It's easy to live in a state of panic. Those walls of water may look scary, but He's the One holding up the walls. God may not deliver you from trouble, but He will protect you through it. Even when life is not peaceful, when you know that He is God, you can trust Him to see you safely through to the other side. (See Psalm 46:1–11.)

———————————⌄———————————

"Be still, and know that I am God! I will be honored by every nation. I will be honored throughout the world."
PSALM 46:10, NIV

54

Power Up

Every morning when you wake up, you need to power up. Get your mind going in the right direction: "This is going to be a good day. I can handle anything that comes my way with a good attitude. I am strong. I am confident. I have the favor of God. I'm excited about my future." At the start of the day, you need to set your mind for victory. If you don't set the tone for the day, negative thoughts will set them for you. Don't let just any thoughts play. Before you check your phone, before you see what the weather is like, before your feet hit the floor, power up with on-purpose thinking! (See Philippians 4:8–9.)

For as he thinks in his heart, so is he.
PROVERBS 23:7, NKJV

55

You Have
the Cure

Two thousand years ago the antidote was developed for everything that will come against you — not by a leading scientist or a team of researchers — by the Son of the living God. When Jesus went to the cross, He took on your guilt, your shame, and your failures. He not only bore your sins, He took your sicknesses. You're not at the mercy of fear, depression, addictions, or other diseases. You have the cure. The Most High God is breathing in your direction. He is with you and for you. Now get up every morning and take your medicine so that you can live blessed and less stressed! (See Isaiah 53:5.)

"Behold, the Lamb of God, who takes away the sin of the world!"
JOHN 1:29, ESV

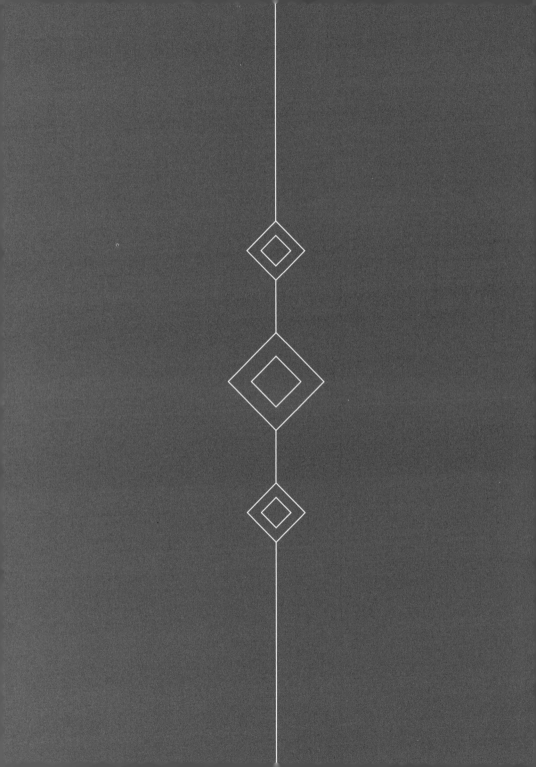

Stay encouraged *and* inspired all through the week.

Download the Joel Osteen Daily Podcast *and* subscribe now *on* YouTube to get the latest videos.

For a full listing, visit **JoelOsteen.com/How-To-Watch**.

 Apple Podcasts

 YouTube